The Ides of March;

THE IDES OF MARCH;

OR,

ABRAHAM LINCOLN, PRIVATE CITIZEN.

BEING A SEQUEL TO

THE END OF THE

IRREPRESSIBLE CONFLICT.

BY A

MERCHANT OF PHILADELPHIA.

PHILADELPHIA:
KING & BAIRD, PRINTERS, No. 607 SANSOM STREET.
1861.

THE IDES OF MARCH;

OR,

ABRAHAM LINCOLN, PRIVATE CITIZEN.

BEING A SEQUEL TO

THE END OF THE

IRREPRESSIBLE CONFLICT.

BY A

MERCHANT OF PHILADELPHIA.

PHILADELPHIA:
KING & BAIRD, PRINTERS, No. 607 SANSOM STREET.
1861.

We read in "Dombey & Son," that when old Sol. Gills had been absent a whole year, Captain Edward Cuttle, Mariner, became so much perplexed, that he resorted for advice to Captain Bunsby, with whom he had the following conversation:

"Bunsby," said the Captain, appealing to him solemnly, "what do you make of this? There you sit, a man as has had his head broke from infancy up'ards, and has got a new opinion into it at every seam as has been opened. Now what do you make o' this?"

"If so be," returned Bunsby, with unusual promptitude, "as he's dead, my opinion is he won't come back no more. If so be he's alive, my opinion is he will. Do I say he will? No. Why not? Because the bearings of this obserwation lays in the application on it."

"Bunsby!" said Captain Cuttle, who would seem to have estimated the value of his distinguished friend's opinions in proportion to the immensity of the difficulty he experienced in making anything out of them; "Bunsby," said the Captain, quite confounded by admiration, "you carry a weight of mind easy, as would swamp one of my tonnage soon."

We read also, in the true story of the United States, that on the 12th day of January, 1861, public expectation in the Senate-chamber hung upon the lips of William H. Seward, the acknowledged mouth-piece of Abraham Lincoln, President elect; and that those lips, then and there, poured forth a stream of verbiage, commonly called *magnificent diction*, which was of the breadth of a newspaper column, and of the length of three-score and ten, or perhaps, four-score inches, and which bore on its bosom the following impenetrable mystery;

"If, therefore, Kansas were admitted as a State, under the Wyandotte Constitution, as I think she ought to be, and if the organic laws of all the other Territories should be repealed, I could vote to authorize the organization and admission of two new States which should include them, reserving the right to effect subdivisions of them whenever necessary, into several convenient States; but I do not find that such reservations could be constitutionally made. Without them, the ulterior embarrassments which would result from the hasty incorporation of States of such vast extent, and various interests and character would outweigh all the immediate advantages of such a measure. But if the measure were practicable, I should prefer a different course—namely, when the eccentric movements of secession and disunion shall have ended, in whatever form that end may come, and the angry excitements of the hour shall have subsided, and calmness once more shall have resumed its accustomed sway over the public mind, then, and not until then—one, two, or three years hence—I should cheerfully advise a convention of the people, to be assembled in pursuance of the Constitution, to consider and decide whether any and what amendments of the organic national law ought to be made."

Our first impression, on the perusal of this paragraph, was that the great Republican had copied after a famous Milesian story, in which a sovereign remedy for the toothache is given, although the narrator chances to have forgotten every ingredient of the remedy. But a more critical examination enabled us to detect the working of the Bunsby mind in the man of Auburn; and we, therefore, hold it to be our duty to render the passage into Bunsby diction, as thus;

"There might be two big States; and they might afterwards be cut up into little States. Do I say there should be? No Why? Because it's against the Constitution. *The bearing of this observation lies in the application of it.* There might be a convention. Do I say there should be? Yes, *one, two, or three years hence.* Avast then, keep a bright look-out for'ard and good luck to you."

Now the Bunsby mind was always in Jack Bunsby, as witness the following opinion antecedent by a whole year to the one first quoted:

"Do I believe this here Son and Heir's gone down, my lads? Mayhap. Do I say so? Which? If a skipper stands out by Sen' George's Channel, making for the Downs, what's right ahead of him? The Goodwins. He isn't forced to run upon the Goodwins, but he may. The bearings of this observation lays in the application on it. That a'nt no part of my duty. Awast then, keep a bright look-out for'ard, and good luck to you."

But the versatile Senator from New York, was not at all Bunsbyish when he said at Detroit, hardly four months before the 12th of January:

"My humble advice, then, fellow citizens, is, that we return and re-establish the original policy of the nation, and henceforth hold, as we did in the beginning, that slavery is and must be only a purely local, temporary, and exceptional institution, confined within the slave States where it already exists, while freedom is the general, normal, enduring, and permanent condition of society within the jurisdiction, and under the authority of the Constitution of the United States."

And also: "Certainly, therefore, we have no need

and no room for African slaves, in the Federal Territories."

No one could find mystery hidden in his language, then, nor was its teaching obscure. Why, then, does he now offer us only a choice between unconstitutional legislation, on the part of a factious congress, and impossible delay on the part of a suffering and excited people? In other words, why did he put on the Bunsby mind, on that momentous 12th day of January?

Grecian mythology is very instructive reading There, for example, is the story of Phaeton. We learn from it, that a certain old Sol, in days long gone-by, required considerable persuasion, before he was willing to hand over his horses and chariot to that graceless young fellow, who, in less than twenty-four hours, set the whole world afire. The crafty boy was full of promises, until he had cajoled the old gentleman out of the ribbons, but as soon as he was on the box and had cracked his whip, we read that

> "The sun's perpendicular rays
> Illumined the depths of the sea;
> The fishes, beginning to sweat,
> Cried, hang it! how hot we shall be"

Now, in Mr Seward's view, a convention, in the present excited state of the public mind, is out of the question This is one horn of the dilemma, which he tenders in the name of conciliation. The other horn is unconstitutional legislation, which may, in due season be reviewed and pronounced void by United States Judges, of Lincoln creation. Does not every one know that the Supreme Court of the United States is principally composed of men who can hardly expect to see another President inaugurated, after the term of Abraham Lincoln?

Now, in our judgment, when William H. Seward

enunciated his mystery of the 12th of January, he sought to be one of those,

> "That palter with us in a double sense;
> That keep the word of promise to our ear,
> And break it to our hope"

It was the cry of peace, peace to the South, with the intention of subjugating its people by subtilty in the end. Or, to speak figuratively, it may be that, like Benhadad, the Syrian, Mr. Seward had drank himself drunk, (new wine of "cabinet brand" is very heady,) and, therefore, cried out in *magnificent diction*, respecting the advancing forces of the South; "whether they be come out for peace, take them alive; or whether they be come out for war, take them alive." It is at least plain that he looked upon his political adversaries as men whom it was easy to entrap; and it is equally plain that the "Benhadad platform" has been soberly adopted by the good people of Michigan, who have, within a few weeks, passed five resolutions, calling upon the Administration to imprison all persons sent to Washington as commissioners from the seceding States, and to resume all the forts which the troops of the seceding States have seized

Since that time Mr. Seward has taken to informing committees of working-men, and committees of merchants, the Senate of the United States, and all other parties concerned, that the negro question, the slavery-extension-question is *nothing*, and that it never can be a practical question, because there is on the average only one slave to a territorial area equal to the surface of the State of New York, but that the great question, and the only question now is *to save the Union.* He would have spoken much more candidly if he had said: "The only question now is, how Mr Lincoln and I are practically to get into office." And is it possible, that this man, who a few months ago travelled from the Atlantic coast almost to the verge of the Rocky Mountains, in order to set the whole land in a state of uncontrollable frenzy as to the negro-question, has now the *sang-froid*, the inconceivable audacity, to assure us that that same negro-question is nothing, after all? We read that whilst Rome was burning Nero fiddled; but at least he kept within his palace. He did not go abroad and make a set speech, to assure the good people that the fire was nothing, but that the question was how to save the buildings of the Imperial City. What is consuming the Union at this moment, but the very fire which Mr. Seward and his coadjutors kindled?

"As a madman who casteth fire-brands, arrows, and death, so is the man that deceiveth his neighbor and saith, am not I in sport?" And again: "It is as sport to a fool to do mischief; but a man of under standing hath wisdom." And now, we ask, under the wisdom of Solomon, recorded in the book of God, what confidence should the people of these already *disunited* States have in the man, whose large natural abilities. together with his great position as Senator from the Empire State, have enabled him to constitute Abraham Lincoln his own particular puppet, to play the part of President from 1861 to 1865, under his own auspicious Chief Secretaryship?

On that eventful 12th day of January, all hope of settlement forsook the minds of the Senators and Representatives of the Cotton-States. Who could not see that the only alternative was to follow the lead of South Carolina and secede, after Mr. Seward had thus stated the foundation of the present crisis?

"The occasion is the election of a President of the United States, who is unacceptable to a portion of the people. I state the case accurately. There was no movement of disunion before the ballots which expressed that choice were cast. Disunion began as soon as the result was announced."

Such, according to Mr. Seward's *accurate* statement of the case, being *the real*, though trivial cause of our present serious difficulties, he proceeds to summarise certain *ostensible* grounds on which, (he says) Southern disunionists have sought to place their platform; as thus:

"The Disunionists, consciously unable to stand on their mere disappointment in the recent election, have attempted to enlarge their ground. More than thirty years there has existed a considerable—though not heretofore a formidable—mass of citizens in certain States situate near or around the delta of the Mississippi, who believe that the Union is less conducive to the welfare and greatness of those States than a smaller Confederacy, embracing only slave States, would be. This class has availed itself of the discontents resulting from the election, to put into operation the machinery of dissolution long ago prepared and waiting only for occasion. In other States there is a soreness because of the want of sympathy in the free States, with the efforts of slaveholders for the recapture of fugitives from service. In all the slave States there is a restiveness resulting from the resistance which has been so determinedly made within the last few years, in the free States, to the extension of slavery in the common territories of the United States."

We pause here for a moment to remark that most men of sound mind hereabouts, think that Mr. Seward's statement of alleged Southern grievances, is open to the small objection of putting the last first, and the first last, and calling the least greatest, and the greatest least; and then we inquire, with all due respect, who is this Abraham, this new father of the faithful, that the Southern people of these United States should so greatly disquiet themselves about his accession to $25,000 per annum, a home in the White House, and the official patronage which may lend him consequence as an individual, or enrich his political associates during four years to come? Does it seem likely that many men of character and property, and many States of great wealth, would rush into revolutionary acts, and a provisional government, with all contingent hazards of civil war, as a possible and only too probable consequence, simply to frustrate Abraham, the *quondam* rail-splitter in the field, the present hair-splitter on the stump, in his expected treasures of office? It is an insult to the understanding of a child to "state the case accurately" in the Seward line of argument. If that be accuracy, most men would rather have such inaccurate statements as the following:

The presidential election of the year 1860 was *constitutional in form, but sectional and therefore revolutionary in spirit.* During the excited canvass between Mr. Lincoln and his opponents, ominous threats of Southern secession as a contemplated counterpart to Northern denial of the rights of slave-holders, were *daily heard by every one, Mr. Seward not excepted.* But he, and other partizan leaders, chose to be incredulous, and to assure the Northern people of the United States that the wolf, called disunion, was not coming out of South Carolina, nor out of any other State. That wolf, however, did come before last Christmas day; but "who's afraid?" said the eminent Republican. Then came the platitudes and the mystery of a "magnificent diction" speech, on the 12th of January; and thereafter went on secession until, in the language of a few plain lines in that speech, the question of the right of secession has given "place to the more practical one, whether many seceding States have a right to coerce the remaining members to acquiesce in a dissolution."

And indeed the matter has already gone much further than what Mr. Seward calls *the more practical question;* for thinking men in the Middle States are already contemplating as an inevitable future the perfect virtual disintegration of these United States, on the fourth day of March, 1861; and their desire is to see how that which will then have become the baseless fabric of a vision can be reconstructed and restored.

The writer speaks by the authority of common sense, for his own Commonwealth, the State of Pennsylvania, which contains three millions of people, (almost as large a population as that of the entire United States in 1776,) which has bread enough and to spare, which furnishes, for peace or for war, as the case may be, nearly all the coal of the sea-board, which has vast manufacturing resources, and which needs only abundant and good markets for the products of her industry. Can any one, does any one suppose, that the Republican party will have all these resources on any terms whatever, to hurl in the name of Abraham the Honest, or Hannibal the Great, or William the Conqueror, in an irrepressible conflict, and in the name of coercion, or in any other name, against the South? Can we not live *within ourselves,* combining ease and dignity in happy proportion, whilst we assure the Republican leaders that our people are not prepared to acknowledge that nineteen thirty-fourths of the United States are the United States, nor that any other fractional part is the whole? Can we not consider inauguration a harmless pageantry, an inexplicable dumb show, in which without the accompanying terrors of Governor Houston's dead body, an *Ex-United* States Chief Justice, with an air of great solemnity, swears into imaginary office, a gentleman whose programme for his first appearance on a very large theatre, is to illustrate the resemblance between the map of the United States and Daguerre's dissolving views of scenery? Is not this coolness of inconsistency on our part, or shameless perfidy to Mr. Lincoln, or whatever else any one pleases to call it, *vastly better than civil war*, especially when we know that we shall be the border State for that war, the place of obvious offence to the whole South, because the *place of resort for fugitive negroes*, the chief point of export of coal, and, therefore, *the point to be secured above all others by belligerents?* Does any one suppose that we are going to be oblivious of these considerations, on the fourth of March? Does any one suppose that we are going to join in the chorus of "the Constitution, the Union, the enforcement of the laws," which, being interpreted, means *coercion*, or at least war by a Northern confederacy against a Southern confederacy? Not at all. We are under no such delusion about popular cries as that which Sidney Smith satirized so pleasantly, when he said to the Irish some such words as these: "Of what use is it for an Irishman to split his throat with crying Erin-go-bragh! Better cry, Erin go bread and butter, Erin go shoes and stockings; Erin go clothes without holes in them." We can say for ourselves, without the help of any satirist, that the Constitution was violated by a sectional election, that the Union has since been rent asunder, and that we have no fondness for "enforcement of the laws," which means a free fight by *our* hands, and on *our* soil, whilst Michigan and Massachusetts, being at equally safe distances from the field of conflict, exhort us "to be strong, and quit ourselves like men."

All the above reasoning assumes that the Border Slave States will make common cause with the Cotton States. How can it be otherwise? What in plain terms are Border Slave States? Obviously they are States which *look to discontinuance of slavery in a future, not very remote.* They have in capability and not in development, interests to which the existence of slavery is adverse; mining, manufacturing and farming resources, which are greatly depressed by the paralyzing influence of slave-labor on every sort of work which the slave is not competent to perform. These undeveloped resources hold out a prospect of greater prosperity in the near future, without slavery, than is now enjoyed by such Border States with slavery. They, therefore, wish to sell their slaves at the earliest convenient day, just as New Hampshire, Rhode Island, Connecticut, New York, New Jersey and Pennsylvania eighty years ago were desirous of selling their slaves. And the States which we have last named, or rather their individual citizens, did sell their slaves, and did by such process of sale, send them into the present Border Slave-States, which in due time relieved themselves in part, and which hereafter must fully relieve themselves of slavery by selling them to the great Cotton and Sugar States, which we already have, and to those Cotton and Sugar States which we may hereafter form in any present or future territory of the United States. But if the existing Cotton and Sugar States are to endeavor to stand by themselves, and without the full cooperation and cordial assistance of the Border Slave States, it is plain enough that the early weakness and immediate difficulties of such an exclusively Cotton and Sugar Confederation will be so great as to indispose their white population to add to the natural increase of their present number of slaves, and such in fact as to incapacitate that white population for some time to come from making further purchases of negroes from the Border States. To whom then will the owners of slaves in the Border States be able to make sales, although they may be under the strong stimulus of a natural and proper desire to attain to such prosperity, as *free* farming, manufacturing and mining States have? Is it not plain enough that the dissociation of the Border States from the Cotton States would deprive the former of their only market for slaves, and the latter of the firm basis on which it might and would be safe or profitable to increase the number of their slaves by purchase from the Border States? Theoretical gentlemen may spin contrary theories, but mercantile life generally impresses upon a man's mind the conviction that he who has an article, which he earnestly desires to sell, is very apt to be found in close association and fellowship with the man that chances to be *the only possible person that can want* to buy the article in question.

Therefore, we say, that *the control of the terms* on which Republican pretensions as to the repression of African slavery in the United States shall be quashed, *does not rest with the Border States.* Their natural position makes them anxious sellers; but they will not be able to sell at all, or at least for many years to come, unless they agree to terms on which Cotton and Sugar States can afford to be prompt and eager buyers. Those terms have already been defined with the most striking clearness and simplicity. The definition will be found in sundry acts of secession, adopted *on the Anti-Republican ground* that the Constitution of the United States carries slavery into all the territory or common property of the Union. Verbal definitions may be obscure, or open to varieties of construction, but when a certain interpretation of any instrument is supported by the public acts of States, ready, if need be, to maintain by force their own interpretation of that instrument, all chance of two conflicting interpretations, or of any verbal dispute in the future, has certainly disappeared from the limits of the incipient

Confederacy, which has interpreted conclusively for itself by such acts of secession. This is the great advantage which actions have over simple speech. Every one may remember that at the outset of the French Revolution it was a favorite point with the crowned heads of Europe to *deny the existence* of the French Republic. A few years later Napoleon, a very young man and only, as yet, General Bonaparte, flailed the Austrians in Italy at such an unmerciful rate, that he drove them, in a few months, into the treaty of Campo Formio. A protocol was drafted by some Austrian of the red-tape school and submitted to the conqueror at Leoben. Its first article acknowledged *the existence of the French Republic.* "Strike that out," said Napoleon, to the scribe, when he began to read his verbiage; "you might as well say that the sun shines." For a somewhat similar reason neither Crittenden propositions, nor Border State resolutions, nor Kellogg propositions, nor any other form of words will be needed by the new Confederacy, which is to have its nucleus in the existing Cotton States. These things would have done very well in their day, only a few weeks ago; but revolutions do not go backward. Of any new form of speech, whatever, we must now say, "It is too late." We all remember the crushing effect of that laconic reply by which some one, without even rising from his place in the French chamber, quietly put aside in the afternoon Louis Philippe's proposal for a regency in favor of his grandson. The very same Assembly had in vain solicited from him in the morning the very same proposition.

Thus it is plain that the Border States must coalesce with the Cotton States. It is also equally plain that the Cotton States cannot require from the Border States a pledge that these last will always remain Slave States.

He who forms new connexions in business, in order to sell a portion of his property to advantage, will certainly not give a pledge to keep to the end of time the very property which he so earnestly desires to sell. Therefore pro-slavery enthusiasts need not indulge the delusion that slavery is to emigrate further South and West, and yet to remain in full force where it now is, to the North and East of the Cotton States And if Border States, which are soon to be Free States, are desirable additions to the proposed Cotton and Sugar Confederation, much more are those Free States, which view the slavery question without fanaticism, desirable as immediate additions to the combined fifteen Slave States.

We turn now to the study of geography "Put up the map of Europe!" said Mr. Pitt, when a great war, involving, as he supposed, great changes of the boundaries of empires, had broken out on the continent. "It will be time enough," he added, "to open it thirty years hence." That war went on for almost the life time of a generation. There was great desolation, immense suffering, but, in the end, no material change of the limits of any of the bleeding, fever-stricken, bankrupt, exhausted empires of the old world. Therefore, fellow-citizens of Pennsylvania and of the United States (we cannot call our country by any other name), let us, as yet in blessed peace, open and attentively consider the map of the United States. We instinctively fasten our eyes on two points, which were shining marks for our British brethren during the war of 1812. The one is Washington—the other New Orleans. We stretch a compass from Washington to the point where the waters of Lake Erie form the shore of the State of Pennsylvania. Our sweep from Erie, towards the right hand, or East, strikes the Hudson river at the town of Hudson, intermediate between Cattskill and Albany, avoids the State line of Massachusetts, and comprises about one-half of the State of Connecticut, striking the coast of the sound half way between New Haven and New London. Our southern sweep from Erie takes in the eastern flank of Ohio, nearly all Virginia, and nearly all North Carolina, striking the city of Wilmington, and almost touching the boundary of South Carolina. More than half of the populations of New York and Connecticut; all of New Jersey, Pennsylvania, Delaware and Maryland, nearly all Virginia and and North Carolina, and a densely populous portion of Ohio, to say nothing of the District of Columbia, lie within that segment of a circle which we have described with our compasses. At a rough guess, we may fairly say that one-third of the population of the whole United States may be found within the limits which we have indicated; and we may add, that not one man, woman, or child, in forty, with fanatical views, *pro* or *con*, in respect to slavery, can be found within those limits. Moreover, the whole of these ten millions of people are inextricably connected with and dependent upon each other, by reason of ties of family and business, by railroad communication, mercantile credits, and the supply and demand of commodities. The circular line, which we have drawn, represents an endless chain, freighted with comforts and conveniences, and revolving inwards from Long Island Sound to Cape Fear. Now why should all of us, crowded, as we are, into what is really a pretty narrow space for this Western Hemisphere of magnificent dimensions—why should we adventure life, and limb, and property, and peace of conscience, and true religion, and every thing else on an absurd, fanatical question about the further extension of African slavery? Every one will admit that the blacks must multiply somewhere. On that point every race has a bill of rights anterior to the Flood, and going back even to Paradise; and we must, in candor, admit that the African race has always availed itself of its rights, and has never fallen short of its duty in the premises. Then, if they must increase, they must have more room. If any one wishes to free them, and put them, as tropical plants, on an equality with indigenous whites, let him devote his private fortune to the purchase; and if he has any reward, it will certainly be "after this present life ended." But if no one has money of his own to spare in this wise, let us not withhold from the humble toil of the cotton-picking African that national domain, which is now partly a barren desert and partly a wilderness of prairie or of forest. Let us not talk fanatically about the pollution of virgin soil by the foot of the overseer. That virgin soil, about which politicians declaim with affected fervor, is, in the estimation of common sense, nothing but "the wilderness and the solitary place," which would be glad of any population whatever. Let us, therefore, cease from such ranting; and let us, in lieu thereof, entreat Almighty God that our populous cities be not blackened by the smoke of battle, nor our fertile fields trampled, in our day, by the feet of opposing armies, and fattened for our children by the blood of men, who died in the very act of fratricide.

And now we place one point of our compasses at New Orleans, and we extend the instrument until we find that the most north-eastern point of South Carolina and the most north-eastern point of Missouri are equi-distant from that city. The segment of a circle, which we now describe, comprises the seven States which have seceded. It also embraces Arkansas, Tennessee, Kentucky, the city of Cincinnati, in Ohio, and those portions of the States of Indiana and Illinois which have their natural outlets by the mouth of the Mississippi. In our enumeration of contents, we should not omit the western portion of North Carolina, a small fragment of Virginia, a slice of bleeding Kansas, with Lecompton written upon it, and the whole of the Indian Territory. Here, again, in a segment of a circle, we find about ten millions of people, who must have close relations with each other, and must constitute another endless chain, composed of links of family and ties of business, so long as cotton has a market for cash, and even so long as the rivers of our West shall run towards the father of waters, and the father of waters himself shall wander listlessly and lazily toward the Gulf. Indeed, we may say that until negroes shall have ceased to pick cotton, and eat corn and hogs, there cannot be any great hostility between the men of Cincinnati and the men of New Orleans. Their disputes will limit themselves to points concerning bags and bales, or concerning barrels and hogsheads. The extension or non-extension of slavery is a question with which rich districts, needing a good near market, as well as an outlet by the Mississippi, cannot afford, and will not under take seriously, or, at least, permanently, to intermeddle.

Now, what portion of the United States is outside of our two segments of circles? California and Oregon of course. They will give their adhesion and their wealth to the highest bidder; and we, therefore, conclude that if our two several segments of circles are harmonious, each within itself, and mutually towards each other, there will be no strong attraction to draw the wealth of the Pacific from the "Reformed" United States.

As for Utah, be it far from us to claim it as an honorable appendage! New Mexico and Washington Territories are very magnificent, without doubt, in the way of mountains; but they have not much population to enjoy the prospect. We confess, also, that we shiver at the thought of Pike's Peak, the Black Hills, and the Devil's Lake, which, respectively, lend their charms to the western part of Kansas, to Nebraska, and to Dacotah. We feel as if we had gotten back to the resorts of man, when we look at Minnesota, Iowa, Wisconsin, and Michigan. These are, we confess, incendiary States. It is necessary to warm up one's blood, at times, when a man resides in such high latitudes. They are, therefore, particularly warlike at this time, and, perhaps, also, in part, on John Randolph's famous principle of increasing one's words of defiance in proportion to the square of the distance of one's antagonist.

And now what shall we say of those large portions of Ohio, Indiana, and Illinois, which have a lake shore interest? What of Northern and Western New York, which has its shores upon Lake Erie and upon Lake Ontario? What of Maine, New Hampshire, Vermont, Massachusetts, Rhode Island, and Eastern Connecticut? In respect to Rhode Island and Eastern Connecticut, it is easy to show that their dominant interests lie with those Middle and Southern Atlantic States, which are embraced in our first-described segment. The traffic between New London and Providence, on the one hand, and New York on the other, maintains a railroad and several lines of steamboats, in competition with each other. Goods go mainly South from Connecticut and Rhode Island, to the great Metropolis, or to Philadelphia, for sale. Maine, New Hampshire, and Massachusetts produce quite enough for the solid men of Boston to stand up under. The question, the practical question, the only question for these three last-named States, for Vermont, for Western New York, for Michigan, Wisconsin, Minnesota, for

Northern Ohio, Northern Indiana, Northern Illinois, in a word, for about one-fourth of the people of the United States, is simply this: Has your virtue, on the point of slavery gone so far ahead of that of your Revolutionary forefathers, and our Revolutionary forefathers, that you must go off, or, if the word must come out, *secede* from the rest of the Union, and form some sort of new confederation, either amongst yourselves, or with your Lake and St. Lawrence River neighbor, Canada, together with the other British Provinces?

Now you will admit, that by yourselves, as a confederacy of seven or eight millions of people, with plenty of sea-coast, and of manufactured goods, on the one side, and plenty of lake-shore and breadstuffs on the other *very distant side,* you would have quite a chilly and uncomfortable time of it. We, therefore, consider at once the probabilities of your coalition with Canada and the British Provinces.

You may be assured that you cannot have any coalition with those British possessions, unless you can first persuade their people to declare themselves absolved from allegiance to Great Britain. "Verdant Greens" do not abound in the British Parliament, to such an alarming extent, as to make the public mind of the United Kingdom credulous on the subject of the fondness of the sons of the Pilgrim Fathers for hereditary royalty and control by a mother country. There are men now living in the realm of Queen Victoria, who remember that the first trouble of her reign was with the Canadas; and who remember also the burning of the steamboat Caroline, and the presence of General Scott on the frontier to repress interference by the lake-shore population of the United States. In those days the Canadas were expensive and unimportant possessions of the British crown.

Now the dominions of Great Britain on this continent, are no longer burdens on her finances, whilst on the other hand, certain quite supposable eventualities might make them for a time of the highest possible importance to her. Suppose that France and Russia should coalesce for her invasion, aad actually accomplish that direful work, who can over-estimate the importance of British North America to Great Britain and Ireland in such an emergency? Where else in all her foreign possessions, could she build fleets and equip armies to fly on the wings of the wind, or rather with the panting haste of the steam-ship to the rescue of English hearts and English homes?

We, therefore, think that you will not obtain the sanction of Great Britain for any sort of coalition with Canada. We feel equally sure that Canada and the other British Provinces will not revolt from an easy, absent sovereign and pass into a new confederation, in which you would certainly have the upper hand, and which from the very conditions of its birth, would have to be an ambidexter combatant against Great Britain, and the United States. Moreover, we cannot spare you. We love you as brethren. We love Northern fire-eaters just as we love Southern fire-eaters; and besides we should be shorn of a large part of our glory, if the lakes on which we won our naval victories, together with Lexington and Bunker Hill, and even Liverpool wharf were outside of our borders. Come then with us and we will do you good.

"But slavery!" you exclaim. "We cannot abide it. It is an accursed thing!" Very well, we will not argue the point; suppose it is an accursed thing. Do you mean to commit political suicide, in order to get rid of it? We ourselves consider human depravity an accursed thing. We should like to get rid of it; but we have never for a moment thought of laying murderous hands on our own person, in order to accomplish that moral good, which we greatly prefer to the evil that is in us. Neither have we acquaintance with, or knowledge of any persons who entertain violent views against continuance in this depraved condition of terrestrial existence to which we have all been appointed. We find on the contrary, that men who heartily abhor their evil inclinations not only tolerate with calmness their present existence, but even rejoice in the birth of the children whom God graciously gives them. And yet on certain principles, called philanthropic and philosophic, the birth of a child is the extension of an accursed thing, to wit: of human depravity.

We, however, think that even anti-slavery philanthropists and philosophers would readily and warmly answer any apparent angel of light, who should come from Jupiter or from some other first-class planet, to demonstrate to us terrestrials the propriety of suicide, or at least of the perpetual prohibition of marriage on this sin-defiled sphere of insignificant dimensions. And we also think that every citizen of these United States should be able to laugh to scorn the senseless clamor of all the humanitarians of Europe as to African slavery, which is an institution that we got against our will, and which cleaves to us as part of our national life. And yet how vastly preferable is that national life of ours to the life of any other people on God's earth!

In our preceding speculations as to the course of things under the approaching disintegration and reconstruction of these United States, we have freely assumed that if we fail to reconstruct, there must be division of States. Let no one forget that the internal harmony, the very unity heretofore enjoyed by each and every State has grown out of that majestic Union, in which we are represented by *States*, and not by independent counties, nor by districts of the East and districts of the West, nor by river-sections, and lake-sections, nor in fine in any other way than as *Commonwealths.* So will it not be in the evil day when a Northern Confederacy and a Southern Confederacy shall have raised their heads in antagonism to each other. Divisions and subdivisions, in sickening detail, will press upon our attention, consume our resources and exhaust our hopes. So will it be north, so will it be south of Mason and Dixon's line.

What then is our obvious, our only refuge from these frightful evils? It is simply to hold ourselves free for passage on or immediately after the 4th March, 1861, into or under some provisional government, looking to a reconstruction of the United States, on the original principle of that union in respect to slavery. That principle needs no explanation, or verbal statement. It has as we have already said, been expounded by secession. To the seven States, which have already gone out of the Union, will soon be added the other Slave States. The repudiation of Mr. Lincoln, by Pennsylvania, will turn the scale against him and *therefore against civil war.* New Jersey and the city of New York will speedily declare themselves in the same sense; and then time and patience, under the blessing of Heaven, will do the needful work of reconstruction, provided we have any capacity for that sort of virtue and common sense, which held our forefathers together by what some men called a rope of straw, during all the dangers and the weakness of our country from 1776 to 1789.

And now we proceed to consider a point, which

without doubt has suggested itself to every one's mind more than once in the midst of the preceding pages. That point is the very question which some one puts every day to some other person, in words such as these:

"How shall we ever be able again to say that we have a general government, *a government of the United States*, respectable in the eyes of Europe and Asia, or even in the eyes of Africa; a government able to protect us in the enjoyment of our property and rights, whether as amongst ourselves, or towards foreign powers? If" continues the objector, "States may secede whenever they choose, and the whole confederation must then disintegrate and take all the hazards of reconstruction, we shall at all times live under such uncertainties that an exchange of our very free and easy institutions for the firm bonds of monarchical government would appear to be desirable. We must strengthen the general government, or else even reconstruction will do us no good," says our honest but mistaken reasoner, in conclusion.

The reasoner, whose language we have just supposed, represents a very large proportion of the population of all the States which have not already gone out of the Union. His reasoning is mistaken, because he has not read aright the history of the Old World generally and of Modern Europe particularly. That history is emphatically the history of strong governments; and what, we ask, have been the consequences and results *to the mass* of those same strong governments, of which our reasoner is so much enamored. Let him, especially, consider Europe during the three centuries which have elapsed since Monarchy, more or less limited, became highly exalted upon the crumbled ruins of the feudal system, and we will easily show him that the history of Europe, during the ten generations of those three hundred years, is nothing but a history of wars, waged without any other real end or object, than the pleasure of the persons who chanced to occupy the chief places of strong governments. It is war and more war, blood and more blood, until blood and treasure being exhausted, peace becomes a sorry necessity of sovereign princes. It is war on account of religion, or war to maintain the balance of power. It is "seven years' war;" it is "thirty years' war;" it is a "war of the Spanish succession," or "wars of the French Revolution," or a "Russian war," or an "Italian campaign." But whatever be the name of the war, the deceased or living statesmen of the strong governments which waged it are the only persons that have been able to see its end or uses. The people fight; they perish by pestilence, by famine, or the sword—it matters little *in what way they perish;*—they lie in the grave like sheep appointed to be slain; or, worse than that, they die with murderous weapons in their hands, and those weapons are crimson with blood, shed, they know not why. It is pitiable to read the life and death of such a man as Headly Vickars, a man of faith, and charity, and prayer, who rose from holy meditation to hew down Russians, and who fell himself in a war for which his writings make no better excuse than an alleged general duty of Great Britain to police the Continent of Europe, in order to keep all its sovereigns within due bounds. It would, however, have been strange indeed if he had been able to produce justification for hostilities, into which the British Ministers themselves admitted that their country *had drifted, they hardly knew how.*

Now it may be a blessed thing for millions of people to be thus at the mercy of a few men who wield *centralized power, or a strong government;* but our preference, (we say it candidly,) is for a government *which shall always be weak, except for defence.* Does any one imagine that the United States, when reconstructed in the manner hereinbefore proposed, can ever be weak for defence? Would not an attack of any foreign power upon our rights bind us together as one man? And what more, in the way of strength, do we ask or want? Is it strength for unnecessary or wilfully protracted wars with foreign powers? The Hartford Convention should have taught us, nearly half a century ago, that we can never have such strength! Is it strength for sectional oppression, or factious internal policy? The Southern Conventions of this memorable winter have disabused every rational mind of the supposition that sectional might can, under the forms of our government, ever prevail over opposing sectional right. We may, therefore, devoutly thank God that we live under a government which cannot venture upon experiments outside of the good of the governed.

Our idea may seem too new to be good; but let no one condemn it without first bestowing some additional thoughts on the history of Modern Europe and on the present condition of that Continent. Perhaps he will ultimately conclude that European philanthropy might be turned to good account if it abstained from interference with African slavery in the United States and directed its efforts to the abatement of "gunpowder slavery," or standing armies in Europe. Our brethren of the Old World deem the innocent and productive enforced toil of the poor African a hardship beyond endurance, an outrage upon the common justice of an age of progress; but they have no words of condemnation against conscription, enlistment, impressment, or any other pleasant device for enslaving a poor fellow for military glory, which yields, as the price of killing and being killed in an unintelligible quarrel, certain magnificent allowances, to wit, clothing, rations, and a few cents per diem for tobacco and amusement.

Returning to our own country, from whose affairs we have somewhat digressed, we wish to add that no one need apprehend that the dangerous experiment of secession, disintegration and reconstruction, will be repeated for amusement, within the natural period of his own lifetime. The process of which we speak cannot pass through its several stages without involving every State of the Union, and every true-hearted citizen of every State, in anxiety and suffering more or less acute. Neither we, nor the children who now sit around our tables, will probably ever forget the discouraging way upon which we have just entered.

We wish also to remark that such nullification of Mr. Lincoln's election as seems necessary for the public good at this time, is virtually an irregular and extreme applition of a process which is quite familiar to Englishmen and which, to their minds, is not only quite legitimate, but absolutely a most essential—perhaps we might say *the* most essential—part of their free institutions. We refer to the *dissolution of Parliament*, whensoever the representation of the popular mind by that body has become a doubtful point. The chief use, and indeed almost the only real prerogative of sovereign power in Great Britain is to send back to the people the men who have proposed measures which threaten the peace of the country. The Crown may, indeed, as every one is aware, simply withhold assent from dangerous legislation; but that is quite obsolete practice. The usage of the present century is *to dissolve* any Parliament which tends to destruction, rather than to edification. Secession, with its natural influences on the public mind, will do for Mr. Lincoln and his Congress, in an irregular way, what Queen Victoria has done more than once, very pleasantly and quite regularly, for the Commons' Parliament within a quarter of a century.

And now we cannot close without calling the attention of our readers to the singular, the frightful disturbance of the whole civilized world at this time, in the name of liberty and civilization. On the third of March millions of Russian serfs will be emancipated. The Emperor has so ordered; the nobility will obey, and the mass, uneducated as it is for such a change, may at once pass beyond the control of Emperor, nobility, and all others in authority. When the British Light Brigade made at Balaklava its memorable charge, a French officer looked on and cooly remarked: "That is very magnificent, but it is not war." We greatly fear that the results of precipitate emancipation in Russia may be such as to justify some one in saying shortly; "that is very magnificent, but it is not civilization."

And then all Europe is at this moment standing under arms in expectation of a bloody conflict which is expected to sweep over Italy, always of course in the name of liberty and civilization, about the opening of the Martial month. And last, but not least, on or about the fourth of March, the people of these Middle States, in general, and of Pennsylvania, in particular, must choose for themselves, between peaceful disintegration in the hope of reconstruction on the one hand, and Abraham Lincoln with civil war, as a humane abatement of African slavery, on the other.

Philadelphia, Feb. 12, 1861.

CPSIA information can be obtained
at www.ICGtesting.com
Printed in the USA
LVHW082304260220
648285LV00014BA/507

9 781362 892809